BP Oil Spill and Energy Policy

A MODERN PERSPECTIVES BOOK

Tamra B. Orr

Published in the United States of America by Cherry Lake Publishing
Ann Arbor, Michigan
www.cherrylakepublishing.com

Content Adviser: Satta Sarmah Hightower, Writer & Editor, Talented Tenth Media, Boston, MA
Reading Adviser: Marla Conn MS, Ed., Literacy specialist, Read-Ability, Inc.

Photo Credits: © Danny E Hooks / Shutterstock.com, cover, 1; © Wavebreakmedia / iStock.com, 4; © ufokim / iStock.com, 5; © ZUMA Press, Inc. / Alamy Stock Photo, 7; © Cheryl Casey / Shutterstock.com, 9, 12, 27, 30; © Kanoke_46 / iStock.com, 10; U.S. Fish and Wildlife Service, 11; © michaeljung / Shutterstock.com, 14; © TTstudio / Shutterstock.com, 15; © Signature Message / Shutterstock.com, 17; © Mimadeo / Shutterstock.com, 19; © Maksim Vivtsaruk / Shutterstock.com, 20; © Ty Wright / Bloomberg/Getty Images, 22

Graphic Element Credits: ©RoyStudioEU/Shutterstock.com, back cover, front cover, multiple interior pages; ©queezz/Shutterstock.com, back cover, front cover, multiple interior pages

Library of Congress Cataloging-in-Publication Data
Names: Orr, Tamra, author.
Title: BP oil spill and energy policy / Tamra B. Orr.
Description: Ann Arbor : Cherry Lake Publishing, 2017. | Series: Modern perspectives | Audience:
    Grades 4 to 6. | Includes bibliographical references and index.
Identifiers: LCCN 2016058629| ISBN 9781634728645 (hardcover) | ISBN 9781534100428
    (paperback) | ISBN 9781634729536 (PDF) | ISBN 9781534101319 (hosted ebook)
Subjects: LCSH: BP Deepwater Horizon Explosion and Oil Spill, 2010—Juvenile literature. |
    Oil spills—Mexico, Gulf of—History—21st century—Juvenile literature. | Oil spills—
    Environmental aspects—Mexico, Gulf of—History—21st century—Juvenile literature. |
    Oil wells—Mexico, Gulf of—Blowouts—History—21st century—Juvenile literature. |
    BP (Firm)—Juvenile literature.
Classification: LCC TD427.P4 O77 2017 | DDC 363.738/20916364—dc23
LC record available at https://lccn.loc.gov/2016058629

Cherry Lake Publishing would like to acknowledge the work of
The Partnership for 21st Century Skills. Please visit www.p21.org
for more information.

Printed in the United States of America
Corporate Graphics

Table of Contents

In this book, you will read three different perspectives about the BP oil spill, which happened on April 20, 2010. While these characters are fictionalized, each perspective is based on real things that happened to real people after the spill. As you'll see, the same event can look different depending on one's point of view.

Chapter 1

Miguel Hernandez

Online Investigator

"**D**id you see those poor birds?" my sister Theresa asked. "They are so covered in oil, they can't swim, fly, or dive." I could tell she was upset. We all were.

Each night, my family and I gathered around the television to watch the latest update on the huge oil spill happening in the Gulf of Mexico. We had been shocked by the horrible explosion at sea and the loss of so many lives. Then, we were appalled at the hundreds of thousands of gallons of oil that just kept pouring into the water day after day. Clearly people were working hard to fix the horrible leak, but it was taking so long—too long for so much of the ocean's plants and animals.

▲ *More than 200 million gallons of crude oil was leaked into the Gulf of Mexico.*

"Every single day, that water is getting more and more polluted, and seabirds, fish, and turtles are getting injured or killed," added my mother.

All of us had seen the photos of the creatures that had been washed ashore after the spill. It was terrible.

"There has to be something we can do," I said, heading to my room.

"There goes Online Investigator Hernandez," said Dad, chuckling. I had earned that nickname months ago because I loved to research and find solutions to problems. So far, my online searching had helped us figure out how to repair the leaking pipe in the kitchen, where to find the gluten-free flour my mom liked for cooking, and how to design a Web site for my sister's babysitting business.

Think About It

▶ Miguel and his family live in Iowa. How does living there change what Miguel suggests the family can do to help? Pick out one piece of evidence that supports your answer.

▲ *In the months after the spill, more than 8,000 birds, turtles, and other animals were found dead from exposure to oil.*

Second Source

▶ Find a second source that describes how human and pet hair were used to help clean up the oil. Compare the information there to the information in this source.

"Miguel, time for dinner!" Theresa yelled from down the hall.

I ran from my room and sat down at the table. My dad immediately smiled when he saw the list in my hand. "All right, Investigator," he said. "What can we do to help with the spill?"

"Well, if we lived closer to the shorelines, we could go right to the beaches and help clean," I began. "Over 30,000 people from all over the country are doing that right now."

"I thought they used backhoes and front-end loaders to clear the oil and **debris** from the beaches," my mom said.

"They do," I said. "But on smaller beaches or those hard to reach, they rely on people for manual recovery." My sister frowned at me, so I added, "They use simple tools, like buckets, shovels, and rakes."

▲ *The coastlines of Texas, Louisiana, Mississippi, Alabama, and Florida were all affected by the spill.*

▲ *The Deepwater Horizon was a rig drilling for oil 40 miles (60 kilometers) off the coast of Louisiana.*

I continued, "Since Iowa is a long way from the Deepwater Horizon drill site, we have to find other ways to help. We can make donations to places like the National Audubon Society or the Marine Mammal Center. They will get the money where it is needed the most. Also, the Suncoast Seabird Sanctuary in Indian Shores, Florida, is asking for items like paper towels, bottled water, bleach, and heavy-duty trash bags."

"I can easily add all of that to my grocery list this week," Mom said, grabbing a pencil and paper.

"Dad, you can really help," I said. "I found out that one of the **booms** they use to soak up oil on the water is mostly made from

▲ *Wildlife rescue organizations train volunteers to clean oil from animals after a spill.*

▲ *There was 5.5 million feet (1.7 million meters) of boom used in the Gulf of Mexico to absorb oil.*

human and clean pet hair." I could tell from my family's faces that they did not believe me. "No, really!" I said. "The hair is stuffed into **nylons**, which are made into mats and then used like a sponge to absorb oil. Dad, you could collect all of the hair from your barbershop."

"Can do, son! I will start filling up bags tomorrow," he said.

"I could sweep up all of the hair that falls off Max," Theresa said, pointing to our very hairy collie sleeping under the table. "She sheds enough to create a boom all by herself!" Everyone laughed.

"Wait a minute, Miguel," my dad said. "We've all got our assignments. What about you?"

"I'm adding all of this information to our school's Web site to see if I can get other families involved," I replied. "Online Investigator Hernandez is on the case!"

Cleanup Job

Cleaning birds covered in oil from a spill is a difficult process. For example, a pelican is first massaged in warm vegetable oil and then submerged in a sink full of dishwashing soap. Each feather is cleaned carefully and slowly, sometimes with a toothbrush. The pelican is dried and then kept safe for a week until it is healthy enough to be returned to the wild.

Chapter 2

Sarah Linfield

California Student

My father turned up the speakers so he could hear the **podcast** better. Every Thursday evening, Dad had a few of his friends over, and they all listened to their favorite 90-minute podcast. Dad explained that the podcast was about stopping the use of foreign oil, focusing on alternative energy sources, and shifting to a better way of thinking. I still did not understand why they found the topic so interesting, but they did. When the podcast ended, the group would talk for hours, and sometimes the discussion would get loud!

Ever since the Deepwater Horizon oil **rig** exploded deep in the ocean off the coast of Louisiana, the conversations had gotten even

▲ *More than 85 percent of the earth's energy is provided by fossil fuels like oil, natural gas, and coal.*

noisier. Our neighbor, Mr. Simmons, talked about what would happen to gas prices now that hundreds of thousands of gallons of oil were pouring into the Gulf of Mexico every single day.

"This oil spill is another example of why we just have to reduce our country's dependence on oil," my dad said. "This constant drilling is destroying our environment. **Tankers** leak, and oil rigs explode!"

"Can you imagine what we might be able to achieve if we had the hundreds of millions of dollars that Transocean and BP are spending to pay fines and clean up this mess?" Mr. Milton asked.

I couldn't begin to imagine how much money and time it would cost to fix the oil spill. The two companies were working to cap the

Second Source

▶ Find a second source that explains how dispersants help and hurt the environment. Compare the information there to the information in this source.

leak. Even so, I knew it would take months or even years to repair the damage done to the beaches, waterways, and wildlife affected by all that oil. It had traveled on the **currents** and been blown by the wind, and soon the oil would reach the shores of Texas, Mississippi, Alabama, and Florida. One news report stated that 1.8 million gallons (6.8 million liters) of chemical **dispersants** had been

▲ *BP's containment systems captured about 17 percent of the spilled oil.*

Analyze This

▶ How is Mrs. Linfield's perspective different from that of Mr. Linfield and his friends? How are they similar?

sprayed from airplanes and helicopters and injected directly into the **wellhead**. Those dispersants helped break the oil down into smaller droplets so they could mix with the ocean water. Unfortunately, these chemicals are also toxic to many types of fish and turtles, as well as to coral reefs.

"Like the podcast said, we have to find a way to invest our money and efforts in alternatives," my father said. "If we could start developing new fuels like Brazil, it would be a great first step." I knew what he meant. At breakfast he had told me that **ethanol** was a fuel made out of corn and that Brazilians were making fuel out of sugarcane.

"Making **hybrid** cars is another step this country has to take," agreed Uncle Simon, my dad's brother. "Let's use electricity, not oil!"

"Just think of the number of jobs we could create if we really pursued alternative fuels and vehicles," Mr. Simmons added. "Talk about economic growth!"

"Hmm," I heard my mother say softly behind me. I turned to look at her. I could tell from the look on her face that she did not necessarily agree with everything the men were saying. "I think your father and his friends are overlooking some important facts. Deep-sea drilling certainly has its risks, as this explosion has proven. But, if we focus on offshore drilling, then we lessen our reliance on Middle Eastern countries for oil. This means the United States could

▲ *Alternative and renewable energy sources like wind and solar have fewer environmental consequences.*

▲ *Gas prices depend on factors like demand and the economy. They also vary based on state.*

determine the cost of oil, not other countries. Gas prices would certainly go down. Offshore drilling also creates hundreds of jobs and spurs economic growth." She sighed. "I just wish more people would remember that there is more than one side to every issue like this."

I left my dad and his friends to their discussion. But their ideas, as well as my mother's, went into the living room with me. Would my future kids one day grow up in a world run on corn or sugarcane? Would they look back at our country's reliance on oil and shake their heads in amazement? Or would they think we should have focused more on offshore drilling to keep costs down? I just hoped that, if nothing else, the Deepwater Horizon explosion would inspire our country's leaders to start making some changes and perhaps even tune in to that podcast now and then.

Then, just maybe, by the time I turn 16, a hybrid will be parked in the driveway.

Paying the Price

The 2010 Deepwater Horizon oil spill resulted in many state and federal lawsuits, as well as countless fines. As of late 2015, the BP Company had settled the majority of them for a total of $20 billion. This money will cover environmental damages and will be paid out over a period of 16 years.

Chapter 3

Abraham Seevers

Louisiana Shrimper

I stood on the deck of *The Jambalaya*. This had been my shrimp boat for the past 10 years, and before that it was my father's. The **trawler** was in tip-top shape because I took fine care of it. I repainted it often, and my shrimp nets were repaired every time I could fit it in. Every morning, before the sun was even up, I checked the engine to see if any valves needed adjusting or if more oil was needed in the engine.

If I closed my eyes, I could see *The Jambalaya* pushing through the Gulf waters, its nets bulging with the day's catch. I could hear the cries of the eager seagulls and pelicans as they followed me to the

▲ *Much of the commercial fishing in the Gulf of Mexico was shut down after the BP spill.*

Analyze This

▶ How does the shrimper's perspective on the oil spill differ from the other perspectives in the book? How are they similar?

shore, hoping I'd share some of it. I could smell the sharp tang of the salt water and taste dried sweat on my lips from the long morning out in the sun. Shrimping was my life, and I wouldn't have it any other way. I loved those squirmy little mudbugs!

When I opened my eyes, the dream ended. *The Jamabalya* was not headed out in search of shrimp. Instead it was tied to the dock, nets folded and put away, and engine silent. When the Deepwater Horizon oil rig exploded and sank last week, my entire world changed. As the oil left the underwater well, some traveled to the surface to form a **slick** and was moved by the wind. Other oil sank down and hung in midwater, moved by the currents. Some oil sank all the way to the ocean floor.

All fishing was stopped. It was not long before more than 80,000 square miles (207,199 square kilometers) of ocean was closed, including my traditional fishing grounds. I've already heard that it will be months before the waters are opened again. But what happens then? I cannot believe this much damage can be repaired in a few months. I suspect that shrimp, along with countless other fish, will

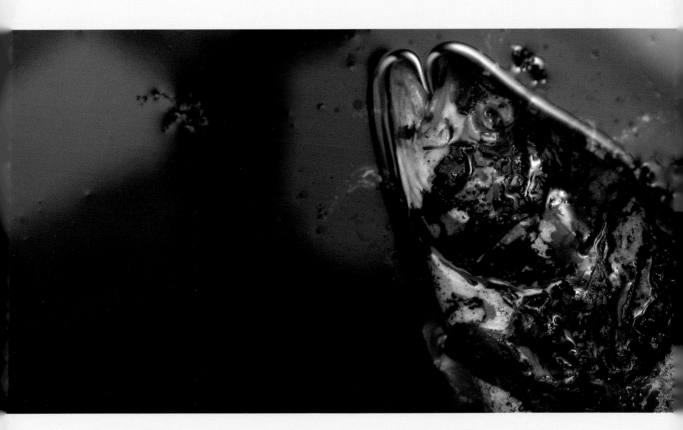

▲ *Oil spilled into ocean waters kills many of the native fish. It can also make fish unhealthy for humans to eat.*

Biggest Losses Due to the BP Oil Spill

Overall cost to the Gulf of Mexico's commercial fishing industry	Up to $1.6 billion
Overall jobs lost in the commercial fishing industry	Up to 9,315
Percentage less shrimp caught in 2010 compared to previous years	65 percent

struggle for a long time to recover from what has happened to their **habitat**.

Even though I did not have much to do with tourism in the area, I knew that it would be a long time before anyone would take a vacation here. Who would want to sit on a beach that has **tar balls** on it or

▲ *After the BP spill, the U.S. government created a $20 billion fund to help clean up after similar spills.*

Think About It

▶ How would a change in a city's tourism affect a business like the shrimper's? Give two reasons to support your answer.

swim in water covered in an oil slick? And most people would be afraid to order any seafood at the local restaurants. No tourism would certainly mean less demand for shrimp.

I put my head in my hands. It was going to be a long and difficult summer. I needed to make some plans. I looked over at *The Jambalaya*. She could use a new coat of paint, and one of the nets looked a little weak in places. I stood up, squared my shoulders, and sighed. It was time to get to work.

▲ *More than 5 million tourists visit Gulf Shores, Alabama, a city on the Gulf of Mexico, every year.*

Look, Look Again

This image shows BP workers cleaning oil off the beach in Florida after the spill. Use this photo to answer the following questions:

1. How do you think other clean up volunteers would feel about this photo? How might they describe it to friends?

2. What would a family who is against drilling for fossil fuels think about this photo? How might that be different from the way a family who relies on the oil business for income thinks about it?

3. What might a commercial fisherman think of this photo? What about a local hotel owner?

Glossary

booms (BOOMZ) floating barriers that slow the spread of oil

currents (KUR-uhnts) large bodies of water moving in a certain direction

debris (duh-BREE) fragments of something that has been destroyed

dispersants (dis-PUR-sents) chemical treatments for oil spills, usually sprayed from the air

ethanol (ETH-uh-nawl) alcohol

habitat (HAB-ih-tat) natural environment of an organism

hybrid (HYE-brid) a mix of two different varieties (such as gas and electric cars)

nylons (NYE-lahnz) stretchy, sheer material often used in panty hose

podcast (PAHD-kast) downloadable audio file

rig (RIG) platform and equipment used in oil drilling

slick (SLIK) thin layer of oil on the surface of the water

tankers (TANG-kurz) large ships used for carrying liquids

tar balls (TAHR BAWLZ) lumps of solid crude oil found in the sea or washed up onshore

trawler (TRAW-lur) a fishing boat used for catching fish with a net

wellhead (WEL-hed) the structure over an oil or gas well

Learn More

Further Reading
Benoit, Peter. *The BP Oil Spill.* New York: Children's Press, 2011.

Brennan, Linda C. *The Gulf Oil Spill.* Minneapolis: ABDO, 2014.

Jakubiak, David. *What Can We Do About Oil Spills and Ocean Pollution?* New York: PowerKids Press, 2012.

Landau, Elaine. *Oil Spill! Disaster in the Gulf of Mexico.* Minneapolis: Millbrook Press, 2011.

Peppas, Lynn. *Gulf Oil Spill.* New York: Crabtree Publishing Co., 2011.

Wang, Andrea. *The Science of an Oil Spill.* Ann Arbor, MI: Cherry Lake Publishing, 2015.

Web Sites
The Mini Page—Environmental Disaster: An Ocean of Oil
www.nwf.org/pdf/Kids/oilspill_mini-page.pdf

National Wildlife Federation—Ranger Rick on the Big Oil Spill
www.nwf.org/kids/ranger-rick/ranger-rick-on-the-big-oil-spill.aspx

Scholastic—Teachers: Oil Spill in the Gulf of Mexico
www.scholastic.com/browse/collection.jsp?id=745

Index

About the Author

Tamra Orr remembers watching the news each night to see if the oil spill had been contained yet. She is the author of hundreds of books for readers of all ages. She lives in the Pacific Northwest with her family and spends all of her free time writing letters, reading books, and going camping. She graduated from Ball State University with a degree in English and education and believes she has the best job in the world. It gives her the chance to keep learning all about the world and the people in it.